SYDNEY

Photography by Geoff Higgins

Text by Dalys Newman

WOOLLAHRA

PREVIOUS PAGE: Flamboyant Greek dancers perform at the Sydney Festival which is held over a three-week period every January and showcases the multiculturalism of the city with an extravaganza of music, dance, performing and visual arts.

ABOVE, BELOW AND OPPOSITE: The Opera House, one of Sydney's best known icons, makes a dramatic statement on the city foreshore. The sculpted masterpiece is sited on Bennelong Point, adjacent to Circular Quay, on a priceless finger of land jutting into the harbour. Designed by Danish architect, Joern Utzon, and costing $102 million, it was officially opened in 1973 by Her Majesty Queen Elizabeth II. It has four main halls for the performing arts, plus an exhibition hall, a reception room and a recording hall. The Concert Hall seats 2679 people, the Opera Theatre 1547, Drama Theatre 544 and the Playhouse 398.

OPPOSITE: Located on the harbour foreshore, overlooking Sydney's bustling Circular Quay, the Museum of Contemporary Art is a centre for the promotion of contemporary art and visual culture.

ABOVE: HMAV *Bounty* was built for the movie *Mutiny on the Bounty*, starring Mel Gibson. This magnificent replica of Captain Bligh's 18th century tall ship sails on harbour cruises every day from the historic Campbell's Cove at the Rocks.

CENTRE: Built in 1816, Cadman's Cottage at the Rocks is one of the few buildings that remain from the first 30 years of the colony. Over the years the sandstone cottage has been used as a water transport headquarters, a sailor's home and a water police station and it now houses a museum.

RIGHT: One of Sydney's finest colonial buildings, Customs House, on Circular Quay, was built in 1885. Designed by James Barnet, it features a clock surrounded by tridents and dolphins and a fine coat of arms.

ABOVE: Fountains and trees create a plaza-like atmosphere in Alfred Street, on the Quay, an area buzzing with ferry and train commuters, sightseers and buskers.

ABOVE RIGHT: Queen Victoria surveys all before her on Macquarie Street. The finest early colonial buildings in the city can be found on this street which shares with nearby Bridge Street the distinction of being the administrative centre of New South Wales from the earliest days.

RIGHT: Centrepoint Tower stands 325 metres above the city streets. It takes 40 seconds for the lifts to reach the summit where there are panoramic views extending to the Central Coast in the north, the Blue Mountains in the west and Wollongong to the south.

OPPOSITE: Built to commemorate the Australian-French Alliance of 1914-18, the Archibald Fountain is the centrepiece of Hyde Park. The work of Parisian sculptor Francois Sicard, it was erected in 1932 and represents stories of Greek mythology.

OVERLEAF: The Anzac War Memorial in Hyde Park was opened in 1934 to commemorate those who served in World War I and is a focal point for Anzac Day observances.

ABOVE: The pyramid-shaped Tropical Centre at the Royal Botanic Gardens houses tropical eco-systems in miniature. Most of the plants inside, including creepers, palms, tree ferns, orchids and bromeliads, come from the wet tropics.

ABOVE RIGHT AND CENTRE: The Royal Botanic Gardens, dedicated in 1816 and reputedly the second oldest in the southern hemisphere (after Rio de Janeiro) provide a tranquil atmosphere in the centre of the city. Situated on the edge of Farm Cove on the southern shores of the harbour, they are an ideal place for the city worker or tourist to relax. It was on this site, in 1788, that the first farm was established to feed the young colony.

RIGHT: The battlements and turrets of Government House make an imposing sight on the edge of the Botanic Gardens. This impressive Tudor style building was completed in 1845 and designed by a London architect, Edward Blore.

LEFT: Spectators crowd the Opera House forecourt during the Greek Festival. This spectacular open-air venue, with the famous white sails providing a striking backdrop, has been used for concerts, site-specific performances and special events such as New Year's Eve. The granite monumental steps provide natural amphitheatre seating and the cobblestone area measures 85 metres x 25 metres, with a seating capacity of 3000–5000. In September 2000 it was the site for the Olympic triathlons.

BELOW: The Art Gallery of New South Wales contains the most comprehensive collection of art in Australia. Works of art on display include a large collection of Australian art, extending from the early colonial period to the mid-twentieth century. Established in 1876, the State Art Gallery originally occupied temporary headquarters, with work commencing on the present building in 1885. The façade, an incongruous mix of classical columns and modern materials, was completed prior to World War I. The names of several famous artists are carved into the stone.

OPPOSITE: Fort Denison, in Sydney Harbour, was originally built to defend the city against a possible attack by Russian warships during the Crimean War. From 1888 onwards it was used to house recalcitrant prisoners who were kept on short ration and the island became known as 'Pinchgut'. It was named after Sir William Denison, then Governor of New South Wales.

BELOW: The 1150 metre long Sydney Harbour Bridge spans the gap between Dawes Point and Milsons Point.

RIGHT: Designed by Henry Ginn with additions by Edmund Blacket, the Holy Trinity Church in the Rocks was built in 1840. It was dubbed the Garrison Church because it was the colony's first military church, being attended by soldiers from the Dawes Point Battery.

BELOW RIGHT: The Rocks market is held every weekend, just beneath the Harbour Bridge, in George Street. A roof of umbrellas houses over 150 stalls offering gifts, antiques and homewares.

BOTTOM RIGHT: Sydney's CBD, seen from Sydney Cove. From a humble and adventurous beginning in 1788, Sydney has grown into Australia's largest and most exciting city.

OPPOSITE: Kirribilli, on the northern foreshores of Port Jackson, is one of many attractive residential suburbs overlooking one of the world's most spectacular harbours.

ABOVE: Hyde Park Barracks, in Macquarie Street, was first built in 1819 to house convicts and prevent them roaming the streets at night. Since then it has been put to various uses, as an immigration depot, an asylum for destitute women and a district court. It is now a museum detailing how Sydney's early convicts lived, and has changing exhibitions of Australian history and culture.

BELOW: The spectacular El Alamein Fountain in Kings Cross is particularly impressive at night. Built in 1961, the fountain commemorates the part played by Australian forces in the siege of Tobruk and the battle of El Alamein during World War II.

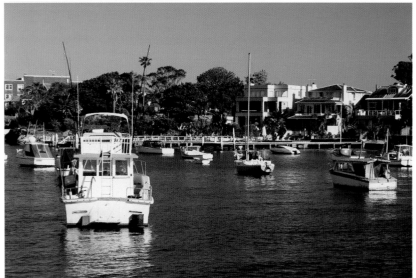

ABOVE AND BELOW: Sydney's Eastern Suburbs stretch from Kings Cross to the coastline. It is a popular and often expensive residential area due to its proximity to both city and beaches.

CENTRE: Famous for its fish restaurants, Watsons Bay in the eastern suburbs retains some of the feel of the fishing village it was in earlier times. The best known feature of this area is The Gap, an extremely high cliff with a sheer drop to the ocean and the site of many suicides.

OPPOSITE: The monorail snakes through the main retail area of the CBD, running down to Darling Harbour before returning to the city area. Opened in 1988, it is one of only a few above-ground rail systems in the world that operates through a major city. A gift to Sydney in celebration of Australia's Bicentennial, it moves over 4 million passengers each year.

LEFT: Sydney's newest transport system, the Metro Light Rail, commenced operations in 1997 between Central Station and Wentworth Park and was later extended to the city's inner west in 2000. Sydney once had the largest light rail system in the southern hemisphere but it was abolished and replaced by buses in the 1950s and 60s.

BELOW: Sunrise over the Anzac Bridge, formerly known as the Glebe Island Bridge. With a length of 345 metres, this bridge is the longest cable-stayed bridge in Australia and among the longest concrete cable-stayed bridges in the world. Completed in 1996, Australian flags were placed on the two tower tops in 1998 and it was re-named the Anzac Bridge to honour the memory of the Anzacs who served in World War I.

TOP LEFT AND ABOVE: With sweeping views of the harbour and city skyline, the huge, world-class Sydney Casino in Darling Harbour is open 24 hours a day and is popular with both tourists and locals. New South Wales' only casino, it operates 1500 slot machines, a TAB lounge and sports bar, Star Keno and 200 gaming tables. The main gaming floor covers 145 000 square metres. Escalators set in a stunning waterfall create a spectacular entrance to the building.

ABOVE LEFT: A kaleidoscope of lights reflect on the waters of Darling Harbour at night. A former dockside area, the small harbour has been converted to a major tourist site and leading convention and exhibition centre.

LEFT: Sydney Aquarium, situated at Darling Harbour over-looking Sydney's CBD, is one of the largest aquariums in the world with over 5000 different Australian fish displayed in their natural habitats.

TOP LEFT: The Chinese Garden of Friendship at Darling Harbour was a gift to Sydney from its Chinese sister city of Guangdong to celebrate the Australian Bicentenary. Embodying principles dating back to the 5th century, the gardens are a haven of tranquillity with their lakes, waterfalls, pavilions, a Dragon Wall and a Chinese tea centre. One of the few public traditional Chinese gardens outside China, they offer a rare insight into Chinese traditions and culture.

LEFT: Surrounded by banks and offices, Martin Place is Sydney's largest pedestrian precinct. It is noted for its interesting buildings, colourful floral displays, and bandstand and amphitheatre that provide regular entertainment for city office workers. Made into a traffic-free area in 1971, it houses some of the grandest buildings in Sydney including the Venetian style GPO. It also features the Cenotaph, a war memorial to World War I servicemen.

LEFT, BOTTOM LEFT AND OPPOSITE: The huge Romanesque Queen Victoria Building (QVB) was designed by Scottish architect George McRae and erected in 1893 to celebrate the jubilee of the reigning queen. Originally used to house the city markets, it is now an exclusive shopping gallery. The open-tiered interior of the recently restored sandstone building features the 4.5 x 3 metre Royal Clock, built in the shape of Balmoral Castle, an original 19th century staircase, vivid red, blue, white and ochre mosaic floors, curving wrought-iron balustrades and glorious stained glass windows. The QVB with its mighty centre dome, consisting of an inner glass dome and an exterior copper-sheathed dome, fills an entire city block.

OPPOSITE: One of Sydney's best-loved icons, the Town Hall is the seat of the city government and the venue for meetings of the Sydney City Council. Italian Renaissance in style, its clock is a popular landmark and the marble steps leading up to its entrance one of the city's favourite meeting places. It features a magnificent wood-lined concert hall, an 8000-pipe grand organ and magnificently crafted stained glass windows.

TOP RIGHT: Built in 1883, the Parramatta Town Hall occupies the site of Parramatta's first vegetable markets. Founded in 1788, Parramatta was the second settlement established in New South Wales. Governor Phillip named the town after an Aboriginal word said to mean 'head of the river' or 'the place where the eels lie down'.

RIGHT: The Parramatta River provided easy access for early settlers to open up the rich agricultural area surrounding it. This area became the first true farming community in New South Wales, forming the basis for the country's wheat and sheep industries.

RIGHT: The first seat of Australian parliament, Old Government House is located in Parramatta Park. Built in 1799, it is Australia's oldest public building. Initially built as a country retreat for the early governors, it fell into disuse in 1845 with the completion of the new Government House in Sydney. Restored by the National Trust, it is now open to the public.

RIGHT: Built in 1793, Elizabeth Farm is the oldest house in Australia. Situated in Parramatta, it belonged to the farming pioneer John Macarthur and was the site of the earliest experiments in merino wool production.

OVERLEAF: Fireworks light up the Opera House and Harbour Bridge during a New Year's Eve display.

ABOVE: Sydney Harbour Bridge is the world's largest steel arch bridge and, with its 49 metre wide deck, the widest longspan bridge in the world. Its total length, including approach spans, is 1149 metres and its arch span is 503 metres. It carries eight vehicle lanes, two train lanes, a footway and a cycleway.

BELOW LEFT: Seen from the top of the south-east pylon, the Bradfield Highway which crosses the Harbour Bridge is, at 2.4 kilometres long, the shortest highway in Australia. Magnificent city vistas can be enjoyed from the lookout on top of this pylon.

BELOW RIGHT: The historic Rocks area is dwarfed by the Harbour Bridge. Affectionately known as 'the coathanger' the bridge was opened to traffic in 1932. The construction cost amounted to $19.1 million.

OPPOSITE: Seen from the Lavender Bay wharf, the Sydney Harbour Bridge connects the city of Sydney to the North Shore.

OPPOSITE: One of Sydney's top tourist attractions, the Rocks area was the site of Australia's first European settlement. Here, on the western shore of Sydney Cove, on 26 January 1788, the convicts and marines from the eleven ships of the First Fleet landed. Cobbled courtyards, catheads and chimney pots, shingles and slates and wonderful old buildings create a fascinating area in the middle of a modern city.

ABOVE: Sunset silhouettes the Harbour Bridge and Opera House, renowned international symbols of Australia.

ABOVE RIGHT: Uninterrupted views of Sydney can be enjoyed from the public ferries that ply the waters of Port Jackson. Regular services leave Circular Quay for a number of destinations within the harbour and associated waterways.

RIGHT: The Parramatta River flows into Port Jackson near the suburb of Drummoyne, with Five Dock Bay in the background. With many sailing and rowing clubs in the area and an extensive harbour foreshore, this is a favourite location for waterfront lifestyle.

ABOVE: Stadium Australia, at Homebush Bay, the largest stadium ever built for the Olympic Games, became famous during the 2000 Olympics as the home of the opening and closing ceremonies and the athletics events. It now hosts Rugby League, Rugby Union and Soccer matches.

CENTRE LEFT: Another Olympic Games competition venue, the Sydney Aquatic Centre at Olympic Park in Homebush Bay was opened in 1994. Since then it has welcomed over 9 million visitors, making it the second largest sporting venue, in terms of attendances, behind the Melbourne Cricket Ground.

BOTTOM LEFT: Manly Wharf is gateway to one of Sydney's leading seaside resorts. Manly was named by Governor Phillip, who recorded that on his landing near the site of the present wharf he was impressed by the manly bearing of the Aborigines.

OPPOSITE: Lined with Norfolk Island pines, the sweeping sands of Manly Beach attract all types of sunworshippers. Located at the northern tip of the entrance to Sydney Harbour, Manly has a natural harbour beach with shark proof pool on one side and one of the city's largest ocean beaches on the other.

LEFT AND BELOW: Sydney is world famous for its beaches, unspoilt expanses of golden sand and sparkling surf. There are 34 ocean beaches in all, including Tamarama Bay in the eastern suburbs (left) and Queenscliff, north of the city (below). Some beaches, with vigorous surf, are for experienced surfers only while others are so tranquil that they are ideal for children and family picnics. Major beaches are patrolled by surf lifesavers during the summer season. The early settlers made little use of these inviting ribbons of sand. Bathing in the open was forbidden between sunrise and sunset until 1902. After this, Sydney's beaches became the village green of summer social life, with the world's first surf lifesaving club being opened at Bondi in 1906.